MW00831795

Publisher: Turtesca Group LLC
Date: March 31, 2020
Place: Pasadena, CA

It's Not Drama, It's Vicarious Trauma

Recognizing and reducing secondary traumatic stress.

Theresa Reed, M.Ed

Limits of Liability and Disclaimer of Warranty

The author and publisher shall not be liable for your misuse of this material. This book is strictly for informational and educational purposes.

Warning – Disclaimer

The purpose of this book is to educate and entertain. Neither the author nor publisher guarantee that anyone following these techniques, suggestions, tips, ideas, or strategies will become successful. The author nor publisher shall have neither liability nor responsibility to anyone concerning any loss or damage caused, or alleged to be caused, directly or indirectly by the information contained in this book.

ISBN: 978-1-7345679-0-8

Promotional Access

Thank you for purchasing *It's Not Drama, It's Vicarious Trauma*. You have now joined an elite group of professionals, caregivers, and advocates dedicated to improving the lives of children, youth, young adults, and adults who have experienced the foster care system.

Please send me an email or visit my website. As a thank you for purchasing the book, please visit my website and sign up to access:

- a free download of the e-book
- exclusive access to on-line workshops
- a free thirty-minute consultation on implementing trauma-informed principles within your agency
- discounted workshop/book signing fees

Books are available for purchase on Amazon.com and on my website.

Best wishes,
Theresa Reed
Website: **www.TheresaReed.org**
Email: TheresaReed@outlook.com
Like and follow me on social media:
Theresareed
itsnotDrama Itstrauma or   @itsnotDramaitsTrauma
@itsnotdramaits

Other titles available:

It's Not Drama, It's Trauma is a series of books focused on enlightening readers on the effects of trauma and the examination of behaviors that may be deemed as dramatic to but are manifestations of a trauma past.

AVAILABLE NOW ON AMAZON

It's Not Drama, It's Trauma: From a foster youth to foster youth- there's nothing wrong with you, you are F.I.N.E.

This edition is presented by a former foster youth, now Author, to help foster youth find their voice by examining their journey in foster care to create a story. The author shares her experiences to encourage other foster youth to rise above the labels and past hurts to know you are F.I.N.E. and will be fine.

AVAILABLE ON AMAZON May 2020

It's Not Drama, It's Trauma: Have You Considered it May Be Reactive Attachment Disorder or Oppositional Defiance Disorder?

Sometimes the impact of trauma is severe enough that a child manifests signs and symptoms of either reactive attachment disorder (RAD) or oppositional defiance disorder (ODD). This volume details each disorder, the importance of proper diagnoses and offers strategies for regulating behaviors.

AVAILABLE ON AMAZON SUMMER 2020

It's Not Drama, It's Trauma: Using math as a strategy for trauma-informed engagement with foster youth and other children with mental illness.

This edition formulates strategies as a play on a mathematical equation. Variables include the 5 Love Languages and the 4 goals of misbehavior Just as math can be challenging without the proper interventions, working with children labeled in school as emotionally disturbed can also be overwhelming.

AVAILABLE ON AMAZON SUMMER 2020

About The Author

Theresa Reed is a Facilitator of Learning who was born in Pasadena, California. She is the Director of Training for Turtlesea Group, LLC and works with many organizations, colleges, and K-12 school districts to provide trainings specializing in trauma, foster care and mental health. She has also been the Program Director for the Foster/Kinship Care Education and Resource Family Approval, and STARS Advisor to foster youth at Pasadena City College for 14 years. Ms. Reed holds degrees in economics with a specialization in social behavioral science from CalState Los Angeles, a master's degree in education with an emphasis on adult education from the University of Phoenix, thanks to a scholarship from the National Foster Parent Association, and is pursuing her EdD, in higher education and adult learners from Walden University.

For over 19 years, Theresa has been a facilitator for foster parent, foster youth, social workers, parent inmates, other parenting groups, group homes, colleges, universities, and a variety of social service agencies and conferences. She is certified as a Mental Health First Aid Instructor in both youth and adult curriculums and in Attachment, Regulation and Competency through the Trauma Center.

Entering the foster care system at the age of 13 was both a challenge and an opportunity. Beginning a new life as a teenager is not the most optimal time to build a trusting relationship. From this adversity, Theresa saw an opportunity to get an education and later began a path toward helping other foster youth. Her years in the foster care system have been the inspiration to begin writing this series of books to encourage and aid foster youth and those supporting them. Among her many accomplishments, Theresa is most proud of her role as mother of two and grandmother of one.

Table of Contents

HANDOUTS

Dedications

It's Not Drama, It's Vicarious Trauma is dedicated to the champions who work with, support or care for those who have experienced trauma.

Dear champion,

Thank you for having the heart to help others. You may be a therapist, counselor or other mental health provider, a social worker, medical provider, teacher, principal, peer advocate or even a caregiver. My apologies if I missed listing anyone. Whatever role you play, this book is dedicated to you for the tireless efforts you expend to support those who are the most vulnerable because of their trauma past. To provide the level of care needed, I am aware that you give of yourself and you take on a little bit of their stories and experiences with each interaction. However, as you do this and take on these pieces and empathize with them, it can cause you to experience signs and symptoms of trauma yourself.

I hope you find this book it to be illuminating to know that someone acknowledges the work that you do takes strength and character. I also hope that it provides strategies that are comforting so you can continue to do the work that you have been so passionate about.

I applaud you for implementing trauma-informed principles with those you are caring for. I encourage you to also be mindful and practice being trauma-informed with yourself. This includes taking care of yourself first and regularly.

Dear Foster/Resource Parent,

You are my inspiration for writing the series, *It's Not Drama, It's Trauma*. This edition, *It's Not Drama, It's Vicarious Trauma*, is a special dedication to you. While the content her is applicable to anyone who interacts with survivors of trauma, the role you play in the life of children in foster care is that of the unsung hero. An unsung hero is "a person who achieved great things or committed acts of bravery or self-sacrifice yet is not celebrated or recognized."

As is my practice during foster/resource parent workshops, I say **"THANK YOU,"** to each of you. As a former foster youth, I am appreciative of my foster parents, the Brockmans. In your role (not job) as a parent, you do not hear thank you as often as you should. I know you do not self-sacrifice for the purpose of receiving the acknowledgement. So, **thank you** for opening your heart and home to care for a child you did not birth and do not have a full disclosure of their trauma history. **Thank you** for the sleepless nights trying to calm a child with night terrors. **Thank you** for not taking it personal when are threatened, accused you, verbally abused and/or assaulted by a child who has only learned hurt, so that is what they give. **Thank you** for co-parenting with the DCFS, judges, attorneys, CASAs, uncooperative birth families, therapists, residential treatment facilities, psychiatric hospitals, wrap around, Department of Mental Health, and anyone else who is supposed to be teaming with you. **Thank you** for fighting aka advocating for the rights of and proper treatment for children who may be diagnosed with some severe psychological disorders.

Navigating these relationships can be physically, financially, and emotionally exhausting and traumatizing. I hope this book can provide you the armor to protect yourself as you continue to fight!

How To Use This Book?

Consistent with formatting from my other books, I provide detail headings in the table of contents for ease of navigation. This book is divided into three major chapters:

1. **Defining it** - We often use words out of habit but have not examined what they mean. I have become a walking thesaurus. In this chapter, I break down terms and share research or data to illustrate the information from a more scientific viewpoint to validate my assertions.

2. **Connecting it** - I will use analogies, scenarios, and visuals to sway an empathetic view of the connection between trauma, stress, your role as caregiver or worker in the helping profession, and consequences for lack of attunement to second-hand shock.

3. **Applying it** - I present activities for you to complete. These activities are to encourage you to reflect on or practice the knowledge gained in the previous chapters.

Each chapter will begin with:

My story - Here, I am taking the opportunity to be vulnerable and share pieces of my personal story as an emotional appeal to illuminate the topic we are about to discuss.

Unlike the first book, this volume is intended to function more like a workbook. I have added more activities to promote reflection. My hope is you will use these activities to process the information and develop goals to stimulate your well-being.

Defining It

Drama vs. Trauma

I would like to posit that even a dramatic response is rooted in trauma. A person who needs to resort to extreme measures to get attention, believes it is necessary because at some time their request for help went unanswered and a need was unmet, leaving them traumatized.

My Story: The Rose Parade

Ok, so for those of you familiar with the Rose Parade, you may be asking, "What does the rose parade have to do with vicarious trauma?" Let me tell you what happened. I work for Pasadena City College on the campus that provides parking for those who wish to view the floats after the parade. Several years ago, I came to work unaware of these arrangements and headed to my usual parking location. Before I could proceed down the driveway, I was unpleasantly intercepted by a volunteer who was serious about their assignment. He stepped in front of my car and proclaimed, "You cannot access this area." We went through a few rounds of me pointing to my staff parking permit and then to the small lot they were not using. Eventually, I declared, "I have work to do so, I am going to park my car and I am not paying for parking today." While this may seem petty, the confrontation was distressing for me. So, as a result, I take extended vacation days after New Year's Day, so I do not contend with the congestion nor the attitude.

What Is Drama?

Since the title of the book is *It's Not Drama, It's Vicarious Trauma,* before I can talk to you about what trauma is, I need to discuss what drama is. The dictionary defines drama as "a way of relating to the world in which a person consistently overreacts to or greatly exaggerates the importance of a benign event." Drama may also be described as sensationalizing an action to achieve an effect. Typically, "drama" is used intentionally whereas a traumatic response is not something that can be controlled.

A comparative example is the aftermath of a car accident where a driver was not paying attention in Los Angeles gridlock traffic, moving at ten miles per hour on the freeway and rear-ended another car.

- **Dramatic response**: The driver who was hit opens their car door and falls to the ground, holding their neck and yelling "whiplash!"

- **Traumatic response**: The driver is too shaken to steer their car to the side of the road.

The dramatic response is performed to give the impression that extensive damage has occurred in hopes of receiving compensation. Unfortunately, I have suffered from whiplash. With the pain that happens naturally, most people are not thinking of throwing themselves to the ground.

What Is Trauma?

There are so many ways to define trauma. For this book, we will us the following definition: a type of injury to the mind that occurs as a result of a severely distressing event. It is often the result of an overwhelming amount of stress that exceeds one's ability to cope, or integrate the emotions involved with that experience." What is considered as distressing will vary from person to person and event by event. When we are healthy, physically, emotionally, and mentally, we are typically able readjust or regulate our responses to ongoing demands. I think a definition of stress is apropos.

What Is Stress?

Stress is a condition or feeling experienced when a person perceives that demands exceed the personal and social resources the individual is able to mobilize. Family, work, relationships, all demand our attention. When you are not healthy or regulated, then life's demands can cause you to feel stressed or excessive demands leads distress.

Stress is a feeling of emotional or physical tension. It can come from any event or thought that makes you feel frustrated, angry, or nervous. Stress is your body's reaction to a challenge or demand. In short bursts, stress can be positive, such as when it helps you avoid danger or meet a deadline.

Have you ever had a day at work that was so stressful you are not able to mobilize the resources to tune out the kids' typical bickering in the backseat? What did you do differently? Maybe you were curt when the children asked you a question or maybe you not-so-kindly insisted everyone play the "quiet game" or maybe you were so numb you could not engage in conversation. If you did anything remotely close to the things I listed, you were stressed.

Here is a visual that I think illustrates this well.

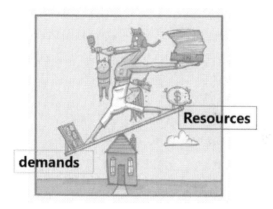

For those who work with or care for others who have been exposed to trauma, prolonged stress from the workplace or consistent engagement can lead to second-hand shock aka secondary stress injury.

Take a moment to complete the following chart:

Demands vs Resource	
Daily demands (ie., work)	Resources to meet demands (ie., education, rest, flexibility)

Activity: To-Don't List

Instructions: On a post-it note, write a list of things that happened throughout your workday that may keep you distracted on your ride home or cause you not to be fully present when you arrive home. Leave this list at your desk. This is your "to-don't" list, these are things not to do or think about during your personal time.

Secondary Trauma

What Is Second-hand Shock?

Second-hand shock syndrome is more commonly referred to as secondary stress injury. But what is it you ask? Good question. It is a cluster of disorders that primarily affect those in helping professions or roles. Because of the empathy needed in these roles, the helper can

Empathy defined

inadvertently absorb the stressful feelings of a directly traumatized person.

em·pa·thy

The action of understanding, being aware of, being sensitive to, and vicariously experiencing the feelings, thoughts, and experience of another of either the past or present without having the feelings, thoughts, and experience fully communicated in an objectively explicit manner

The presence of symptoms of secondary stress injuries affects your empathy and compassion for others, which is the heart of what brings you into the helping profession. Compassion fatigue, secondary traumatic stress, and vicarious trauma are the three disorders that fall under the category of second-hand shock syndrome. Let's examine each of these.

- **Compassion fatigue** is a form of emotional and physical exhaustion. It shows up as desensitization to trauma stories, escalating to apathy and professional inadequacy. Apathy not only affects the way a professional handles a victim's situation, but it can also affect the victim if he or she senses the listener's indifference. Those struggling from compassion fatigue are known to have higher rates of depression and anxiety disorders, stress leaves of absence, and degradation of the work environment.

This fatigue ultimately influences your home life by decreasing empathy and the ability to connect to loved ones and friends.

- **Secondary traumatic stress** occurs when the professional indirectly experiences trauma after listening to the story of others. Your body internalizes what you may have heard and begins to react as if you lived through the event. Some of these reactions include hyperarousal, avoiding reminders or triggers, and even functional impairment.

- **Vicarious trauma** occurs after intensely empathizing with a trauma survivor following discussing the survivor's experience. The feelings can be so powerful that an individual integrates the survivor's trauma into his or her own life. Symptoms can manifest despite attempts of professionals to control their feelings. They can lead to a negative self-transformation characterized by alterations in spirituality or meaning and hope.

The three disorders can co-occur and have similar symptoms.

Signs and Symptoms of Second-hand Shock Syndrome	
Impairment in: - eating and sleeping - sense of trust - feelings of safety - memory - perception of self - interaction with others - sensory experiences	- nervousness - difficulty discussing emotions - anger / rage - loss of self-worth - loss of ambition - increased sensitivity to violence

Many individuals who experience vicarious trauma tend to minimize their feelings, believing their reactions are unwarranted. If left untreated, vicarious trauma can last for months and sometimes years or often lead to thoughts of suicide. Unfortunately, there is a connection between stress and the symptoms of second-hand shock. Prolonged presence of symptoms may lead to a diagnosis of Post-traumatic Stress Disorder.

Post-Traumatic Stress Disorder

Post-Traumatic Stress Disorder (PTSD) is described as the development of debilitating symptoms following exposure to a traumatic or dangerous event. The intrusive symptoms may include:

- Flashbacks, upsetting dreams, or distressing memories
- Avoidance of stimuli associated with the traumatic event
- Changes in cognition and mood (e.g., dissociative amnesia, negative beliefs about oneself, and feelings of detachment or estrangement)
- Hyperarousal and hypervigilance, or exaggerated startle response
- Irritability or self-destructive behavior

Connecting It

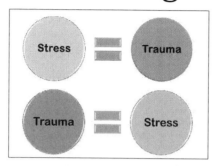

As I was pinning this volume, I reflected on the concept of wide-spread traumatization. In my travels aimed at spreading the good word and reducing the stigma around foster care and mental health issues, I have been privy to many conversations. Some people think we have become an overly sensitive society. The belief is trauma is nothing new. They are correct. However, the reality is, we are being bombarded with the knowledge of traumatic events. Not only are people experiencing greater degrees of horrific traumas, now everyone knows about it. These events appear in the news, blogs, newsletters, and social media posts. People are forwarding, sharing, liking, reposting, and retweeting reports of these events instantly.

We no longer have the luxury of choosing when to open your newspaper and deciding which section to read based on your mood. Before I can log into my email, I am confronted with headlines of disturbing events. Television shows and movies are excessively graphic. They provide no warning of impending images, so we have not time to look away. For some of us, this is traumatizing. It can be especially harmful to children.

I have talked with long-time foster/resource parents who have shared their concerns about the behaviors of our children. I have heard statements such as, "These kids are off the chain and uncontrollable." I retorted with my trauma-informed explanation. I shared that children in foster care are experiencing and witnessing more intensive levels of abuse, neglect, and trauma. I thought of the old saying about computers and data...garbage in—garbage out. Children receive greater levels of exposure to trauma (or input) resulting in exponentially greater responses to trauma (or output) which manifests as extreme behaviors which are difficult to manage. Many are mis-diagnosed and improperly treated, then placed in living situations that cause more trauma, more stress, and exacerbate behaviors. These children show up in your homes, offices, programs, and schools needing your empathy and patience. For you to provide the best trauma-informed care possible, you must guard yourself from stress and being traumatized.

My Story: I Put Myself On A Timeout

Earlier this year, I was so overwhelmed from being empathetic, I had to put myself on a timeout and take some mental health days. During a two-week period, this fall, the demands on my emotional presence exceeded my resources to be emotionally responsive. As I have mentioned, I am a certified Mental Health First Aid Instructor and a Student Advisor for our STARS foster youth support program. In my zeal to provide a much-needed training, I presented or started a total of five different trainings within two weeks. Prior to the start of the training marathon, I consoled a student, I'll call her Vanessa, who had three adolescents who were experiencing signs of mental distress. I encouraged Vanessa to attend one of the Youth Mental Health First Aid courses.

The following week, I checked into the office a bit early with the intent of helping a colleague with some paperwork. While my intent was to be helpful, I got caught in the crossfire of some conversation where I was yelled at and blamed for a glitch, I had nothing to do with. While this altercation was taking place, Vanessa was waiting to see me.

While talking with Vanessa, she was debating whether to drop her class to focus her energy on her children. I told her, school will be here, your children need you now. As she shared the latest situations with her children, I explained that her child's words were an expression of suicidal ideation and admonished her to forego our lunch gathering and immediately get her child to the hospital.

The day following my emotional meeting with Vanessa, I met with another student, I'll call her Ashley, who was in the midst of a mental health crisis. Over the course of her first semester, I was concerned that Ashley was taking on too much, becoming overwhelmed and heading down a dangerous path. While I sat with Ashley, she shared things with me that led me to seek immediate assistance for her. So, I convinced her to walk with me to our Personal Counseling office. Unfortunately, she could not be seen for a few hours. I wanted to have her sit with me until her appointment time but that was not realistic. She agreed to work in the lab until her appointment time. I cancelled my off-site meeting and I told her I would come back for.

Fifteen minutes before her appointment, I returned to the lab to pick her up. I was not surprised but very disheartened to be greeted by staff with a note from Ashley. I felt I had failed her and walked to my car in tears. To pile on the emotional bricks, the person handing me the note, shared the version of the altercation that had taken place in my office, which portrayed me as the villain. This was extremely hurtful. All this in addition to struggling with my statistics class in the doctoral program.

I realized I was extremely stressed and being traumatized by the work I was doing. I went into a shell and informed my supervisor I would be taking a few mental health days. You probably want to know what I did. Well, I got on a plane to spend a few days with my kids in Las Vegas. My daughter asked me why I wanted to spend my time with the "crazies," I told her, I needed to recalibrate my "crazy." They showered me with love, cooked for me, we played paint and sip, and they let me sleep!

I have also made some changes. I will not do so many Mental Health First Aid trainings that close together. I stop offering to be so helpful in matters that are not mine. I schedule more time to spend with my children and I am only taking one class at a time to complete my doctorate. To an outsider, my detachment and subsequent modifications may seem like a dramatic response to typical work stuff. What has occurred is a response to trauma. My goal is to reduce known stressors that I can control.

Major Causes of Stress

When you experience stress, the startle response is activated. This is also called the fight, flight, or freeze response. Stress signals the brain to shift into survival mode to help meet impending demand. Unfortunately, the brain does not distinguish whether the switch was activated because a two-ton bear is present or because of prolonged intense empathy.

Figure 1 shows what happens in the brain when the startle response is activated.

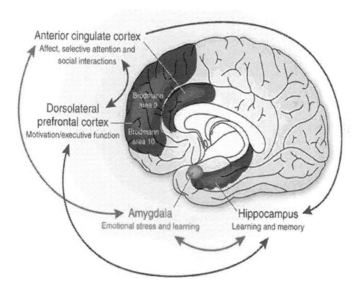

During a stressful situation, the limbic system (the hypothalamus, the amygdala, the thalamus, and the hippocampus) or survival mode is activated, leading to the release of the stress hormones cortisol and adrenaline. These chemicals have a specific destination, a specific time frame to get there, and regulations on how long they are to remain there. After performing their duty when the brain signals "all clear", we are safe, and they get released back into the body. If either chemical stay in the brain too long, it's like having your toilet back up, resulting in damage to other systems. In other words, the brain must recalibrate other systems to handle the excess, potentially overworking other areas of the brain.

Interestingly, stress and learning share the same epicenter. However, they cannot both operate at the same time. So, when you are stressed, you are unable to take in new information. Have you ever noticed how difficult it is for you to pay attention or recall information when you are stressed?

Too much stress causes our survival switch to get stuck in the "on" position. Figure 2 shows what happens to us if we stay "on."

Figure 2: When The Survival Switch Is Stuck "On"

Fight	Flight	Freeze
Loss of temper	Avoidance	Numbing
Irritability	Anxiety	Detachment
Defensiveness	Fear	Giving up easily

Do you easily recognize these behaviors in others? Please review the lists in Figure 2 and circle any of the characteristics that you have shown in the last six months. Your switch might be stuck on.

Some behaviors associated with being stuck in survival mode include the fight response manifested as being short-tempered, even within our closest relationships; the flight response appears as avoidance of people and things you once enjoyed; while the freeze response could lead to numbing and detachment both physically and emotionally. The sufferer may not realize they are exhibiting these behaviors. These behaviors arise from overexposure to stress.

For the helping professional, the list of major causes of stress if vast. Figure 2 shows a graphic depiction of the possible stressors in the work environment.

Figure 2: Causes of Stress In The Workplace

Stress Inventory

Which of these are you experiencing? (please list)

_____   _____

_____   _____

Just as those we serve need support to facilitate healing, professionals need support and consistency. Not only are you being traumatized by the experiences of those you serve, but poor working conditions, interpersonal and intergroup conflicts, and lack of support or supervision from administration can create added burdens. Another stress that is often not discussed is the emotional abuse suffered by champions. Figure 3 presents a list of the ways emotional abuse is perpetrated.

Figure 3: Emotional Abuse

Emotional Abuse				
Constant criticism or attempts to manipulate and control	The use of shaming or belittling language	Withholding affection	Threats of punishment	Isolating someone from supportive friends and family

Emotional abuse is often not a consideration but is equally as devasting as physical abuse. Let's dissect the ways you may be emotionally abused in your role with survivors of trauma.

- **Constant criticism or attempts to manipulate and control.** It Is easy for the outside observer to criticize. Sometimes the criticism comes from the people you are collaborating with. Colleagues or supervisors may be critical in an effort to manipulate you to do things for them such as taking on a particularly difficult assignment.

- **The use of shaming or belittling language.** I have heard of this often from caregivers where they are participating in meeting where the facilitator talks to them as if they have no knowledge or skills. In the workplace, perhaps you made a mistake and your supervisor singles you out in a meeting.

- **Withholding affection.** Affection is the verbal and physical expression of caring. While you may not think of affection in the workplace, the emotional abuse of not being included or appreciated are forms of withholding affection.

- **Threats of punishment.** This action is another form of control. Caregivers have shared being threatened to not have more children placed in their home if they refuse a difficult placement. At work, threats of being written up, demoted, or transferred for unsubstantiated causes is abusive.

- **Isolating someone from supportive friends and family.** Unfortunately, some of the extreme behaviors of the children make it challenging for foster/resource parents to engage with others, and this can be isolating. Being forced to work remotely or not having regular access to a supportive team can be a form of emotional abuse.

Even if there is recourse for the emotional abuse that may have been subjected to, the experiences are traumatic and may have a lasting impact that effects your ability to continue in either your professional or caregiving role. Being aware of how you are being affected can minimize the damaging effects of exposure to trauma and stress. Please complete the activity on the next page to reflect on ways you may be experiencing abuse in your role. After listing the events or situations, please take a step toward healing by identifying ways to promote healing and minimize future exposure.

Activity: In What Ways Have You Been Abused in Your Role as Champion for Those Who are Trauma survivors?

Physically: _____

_____

How has it impacted you? _____

_____

_____

What are you doing to heal from it?

_____

_____

_____

What can you do to avoid re-traumatization?

_____

_____

_____

Verbally: _____

_____

How has it impacted you? _____

_____

_____

What are you doing to heal from it?

_____

_____

What can you do to avoid re-traumatization?

Emotionally: _____

How has it impacted you? _____

What are you doing to heal from it?

What can you do to avoid re-traumatization:

Are You At Risk?

Practicing the essential skill you need to successfully support trauma survivors, empathy, can be a blessing and a curse. As discussed in chapter one, feeling empathy too intensively can make you at risk for second-hand shock. What does it mean to be at risk?

In my Youth Mental Health First Aid courses, I began to examine the definition of at risk. I now refer to is a some being susceptible or vulnerable to adverse outcomes. So, working with children and adults who suffer from the impact of trauma, leaves you susceptible to the adverse outcome of secondary traumatic stress and all its manifestations. There are other factors beside the nature of your involvement that may put you at risk.

Factors such as having a personal history of trauma and the pressure of confidentiality heavily influence susceptibility. Many of you entered your profession or became a caregiver because you wanted to help others who had similar experience as you, this helps you to relate. Those who share commonalities with the trauma survivors they help are more likely to develop vicarious trauma than someone who does not have shared experiences.

Professionals and foster/resource parents are obligated to confidentiality. Taking in the stories or reading the files containing a child's history of abuse without having an outlet to process the information is a volatile combination. For caseworkers, discussing details during supervision in a clinical setting or taking time during staff meetings to do an emotional check-in can be an effective strategy. Support groups or regular meetings with the entire team of wrap-around service providers may relieve some pressure. Consulting a mental health professional for yourself early and often is always a good idea.

> **Food for thought:** Trauma and stress are so interrelated that the DSM has a category - Trauma and Stressor-Related Disorders

Applying It

I SEE PEOPLE THROUGH
TRAUMA LENS

While Trauma-Informed Care is a clinical term, it's not just looking at it from a clinical standpoint of, "Give me all the information I need to know." It is a choice to take in the information and have a different mind-set or perception about what you are seeing, how you respond to what you are seeing, and putting your response into practice. These actions should influence how you greet and treat people overall. This is called seeing people through a trauma lens.

My Story: Stories From The Trenches

Tasha Turned On Me

I experienced the ultimate in betrayal and emotional abuse in the work environment. A colleague, I will call her Tasha, that I have worked with for several years as an advocate for our program cut me deep Shrek. We spent a great deal of time together. She had approached me about serving with her on projects, deferred to me often and complimented me on the work I was pioneering.

Tasha is known in our circle for being a little brash. Sometimes her advocacy was a little over the top and would rub people the wrong way. I recall a few occasions when she made insulting remarks in public meetings where I found myself buffering others from her attacks by redirecting conversations. I never thought I would be the subject of one of her attacks.

After disagreeing with Tasha on an action our committee was contemplating, I became her next target. My supervisor had to intervene and called me in to for what I thought was going to be an update. She shared with me a list of complaints presented to her by Tasha that left me floored. In addition to her negative comments about an event that I coordinated, she attacked the one thing I value the most, my skills as a facilitator. I can only make assumptions as to why she attacked my character. What I do know, is it hurt me to the core.

This unfounded criticism messed with my head for days. My supervisor expressed her disbelief about the tirade. Fortunately, my supervisor was familiar with Tasha's behaviors and the caliber of my work. She advised me to evaluate my workload to diminish my interactions with Tasha. This level of emotional abuse caused me to stop doing some projects I enjoyed, to minimize Tasha's access to me. This type of avoidance is outside of my character but is necessary for my mental well-being.

We need more foster carers, like you.

Caregiver Sally Switches Gears

It had been some months since one of my long-time caregivers, I will call her Sally, had been to a workshop. We shared similar interests outside of the work environment so, I was excited to see her. Over the years, I assisted her with life-skills training and resources for the teenage girls in her care. After class I began asking her about some of the girls she had cared for and she provided various updates. One was on the streets, another went off to college, one finally connected with her birth father. The last story she shared was of one girl who had left and returned to her home several times.

Sally lamented over the emotional abuse she suffered because of the defiance, promiscuous behaviors, threats, criticism, symptoms of severe mental health conditions, and attempts at manipulation from the girls over the years. The last child had been in and out of the hospital several times. Each time she was admitted, Sally would get a call requesting her to visit, coupled with pleas to come back "home," followed by empty promises to do better if you let me come back. I feared Sally was going to tell me she was giving up her license. Fortunately, she has not given up but instead, is now certified for boys under the age of ten. My heart goes out to the many caregivers with similar experiences that have been traumatized while working with foster children. The trauma experienced by social workers is often minimized, ignored or even dismissed as a hazard of the job.

Social Workers On Trial

Unfortunately, as I am completing this volume, the highly emotional and controversial docuseries on Netflix, *The Trials of Gabriel Fernandez,* was released. I am not offering any judgements on the case. However, it addresses the significant flaws in the child welfare system. In my first book, I share my commentary on the system:

> *"In my dictionary, you will see trauma listed as a synonym for foster care."* ~ Theresa Reed

The system continually victimizes and re-traumatizes many of its players. Social workers are among its victims. Charging social workers for falling to prevent abuse is unprecedented. Again, I am not rendering a verdict regarding the actions of the social workers. Director Knappenberger recognizes their culpability:

> *"The social workers took a lot of heat. To some degree, it's warranted,"* he says. *"But that's not the end of the story. There were clear problems with the system they were operating in."*

Additionally, the docuseries notes the long-overdue reform that was implemented to address excess caseloads and the need for retraining of social workers.

Social workers are in the heat of the battle when it comes to serving trauma survivors. Research (and personal knowledge) acknowledge there is a high rate of turnover and burnout. One study classifies indicators of turnover as low, moderate, medium, and high effect. Stress, emotional exhaustion, organizational commitment, and job satisfaction comprise the list of high effect variables. Proposed solutions for the workplace include:

- Addressing stress, exhaustion and job satisfaction
- Refining work processes
- Encouraging better workplace relationships between caseworkers, supervisors, and administrators
- Creating more favorable, trauma-informed work environments.

Social workers are only human. As with any industry but with human service especially, there is the human element to providing service and this same human element is subject to inconsistency and stress from being overloaded. Other professionals are also vulnerable to these same conditions.

Are You Leaving Yourself Vulnerable?

Over the last few years, I have had the privilege of speaking to many middle and high school foster youth about the dangers of commercial sexual exploitation of children (CSEC). During the presentation, I discuss with students to definition of vulnerable and ask them to provide examples of ways they are vulnerable. It amazed and saddened me that youth know they are vulnerable. This book is not about CSEC so I will only share with you part of this discourse as a definition for to examine your level of susceptibility.

Me: "How many of you play a sport?"

Various students raise their hand.

Me: "What type of gear do you wear?"

Students: "Pads, helmets, cups, mouth and/or shin guards…"

Me: "Why do you wear the gear?"

Students: "For protection."

Me: "Protection of what?"

Students: "Body parts that could be hurt."

Me: "You mean the parts that are vulnerable to being attacked?"

Students: "Oh yeah."

The dictionary defines vulnerable as:

1. capable of or susceptible to being wounded or hurt, as by a weapon: a vulnerable part of the body.

2. open to moral attack, criticism, temptation, etc.: an argument vulnerable to refutation; He is vulnerable to bribery.

3. (of a place) open to assault; difficult to defend: a vulnerable bridge.

Are you being wounded in your work? Are you being morally attacked or criticized at work, and it is deeply affecting you? Are you finding it difficult to shield yourself from the effects of the work environment and people? It may be time to replace your protective gear or put on some gear to ward off the impact of working with trauma survivors.

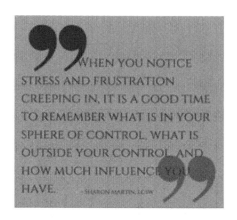

WHEN YOU NOTICE STRESS AND FRUSTRATION CREEPING IN, IT IS A GOOD TIME TO REMEMBER WHAT IS IN YOUR SPHERE OF CONTROL, WHAT IS OUTSIDE YOUR CONTROL AND HOW MUCH INFLUENCE YOU HAVE. —SHARON MARTIN, LCSW

Activity: Assessing Your Vulnerability

Are You Leaving Yourself Vulnerable?	
Behavior	Yes/No
Do you rush heedlessly into stressful situations, then wonder why you feel overwhelmed?	
Do you take on a client/youth without thoughtful consideration of the ways our own issues interact with theirs, then wonder why we feel besieged?	
Do you take responsibility for things you can't control; then wonder why you feel out of control?	
Do you find it difficult to listen to students' stories of challenge and childhood history?	
Do you ignore the warning signs our bodies send us, then wonder why we get sick, develop back problems, overeat, or feel lethargic?	

If you answered "yes" to any of these questions, I encourage you to do some reflection. These items are things you do have control over and can say "no" to when they arise. Your mission after this quiz is to put on your trauma lens and contemplate when you allow these unhealthy practices to take center stage. Once you identify the situations, then you can make a conscious decision not to engage in self-harm.

Regain Your Passion

We have covered a lot of heavy material up to this point. So, I want to take a pause here and thank you again. Even with all the abuse and disappointments you have suffered working with foster children and other trauma survivors, you have stayed the course. I know you did not take on your role as champion, caregiver, therapist, advocate, etc., for the accolades. You have endured stressors that you relegate as part of the job. However, abuse of any kind is never acceptable.

My foster mom used to tell us, "Give me my flowers while I live so I can enjoy them." I wish I could send each of you flowers and a thank you card in appreciation of all you give. Please accept this deliver below from me to you.

As you enjoy your thank you note and flower, I invite you to reflect on why you chose to work with those who have experienced trauma. This will help you regain your passion.

In reviewing research on the cycle of abuse, one of the key factors in breaking the cycle is telling your truth and letting your pain be known. Abuse thrives on secrecy and deception. The emotional abuse we have been subjected to in our work can cause us to discontinue the ventures we were once passionate about. This next activity will aid you in reconnecting.

Regaining Your Passion
Why did you start working with trauma survivors? _____
_____
_____
_____
How did you get started working in this field? _____
_____
_____
_____
What were your hopes when you started? _____
_____
_____
_____

Now, you are let's create a timeline for your work to see how your flame of passion may have diminished over time.

For the timeline, I will give you a few life moments to capture.

Instructions: For each life moment, you will write the year with a tick mark <u>on</u> the line, then write the title or name of the event <u>above</u> the date. B<u>elow</u> the line, you will write how the event made you feel, what areas of your life were impacted, and how. In my workshops, I usually provide a printout on legal size paper. Feel free to hand-write your timeline on whatever size paper works for you. I have a snapshot of my timeline as an example for you.

My Timeline

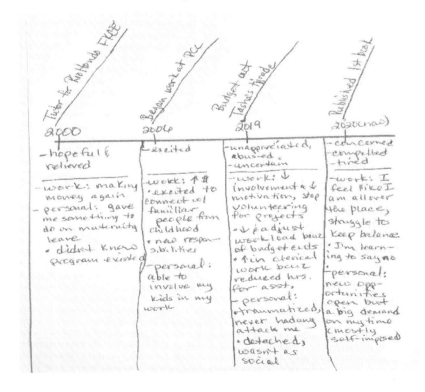

Your Timeline

1. Year you began this work
   a. How did you feel then? How did it impact your work and personal life?
2. Success story or life changing event and year
   a. How did you feel then? How did it impact your work and personal life?
3. List a challenge or life changing event and year
   a. How did you feel then? How did it impact your work and personal life?
4. Today's date (year)
   a. How do you feel now? How is your work and personal life being impacted?

Prevention and Intervention

I am a proponent of prevention and early intervention versus treatment. Here are a few recommendations:

1. **Listen to your body** – we talked earlier about signs and symptoms of second-hand shock, please do not ignore headaches, backaches, and what your body is telling you.

2. **Take a self-care assessment** – this can identify areas of need and offer suggested activities. I have included one in the handouts section along with a list of self-care practices.

3. **Take breaks** – taking regular breaks at work and from work can help you recharge. Learn to spend time relaxing and doing nothing. Use your vacation days. Although you may be saving them to cash out at retirement, if you are not well, you will not be able to enjoy that benefit later.

4. **Forgive** – unforgiveness can hold you emotionally captive. Learn to forgive actions whether they were intentional or not. This does not mean you let people treat you badly. However, if you have been wronged, you may not always be able to confront the offender, or you may not have the opportunity because of time, distance, or death, to ask for forgiveness. So, do not let the need for closure or an apologize eat at you emotionally. I was twenty-five before I finally

forgave my mother for rejecting me. Try using the ritual of forgiveness fire/box/tree.

a. The forgiveness ritual entails you identifying someone you need to forgive or someone you need forgiveness from.

i. For someone who offended you, write them a letter explaining how they offended you and why it bothered you and state "I am releasing you from the hurt I have felt, and I forgive you." End the letter by declaring to yourself that you are letting it go and will no longer allow the hurt/disappointment to impact.

ii. For someone you offended, write a letter acknowledging what you did or think you did, sincerely apologize (no blanket "I'm sorry) and ask them to forgive you. End the letter by declaring to yourself that you are letting it go and will no longer allow the action or inability to resolve the issue to impact you.

   iii. For yourself, are you lamenting over a failure, wrong decision, costly mistake, not taking care of yourself? Then write yourself a letter of forgiveness. End the letter stating what you will do differently.

  b. Once you have written the letter, you can release it ritualistically by either safely burning it, burying it, tearing it and putting it in the trash or mail your forgiveness letter to yourself. At work, maybe you can start a forgiveness ritual.

5. **Unplug** – we are slaves to technology. Try unplugging by turning your phone off at night, schedule (and stick to it) times to check emails and social media.

6. **Guard your mind** – be mindful of what you read, watch and listen to. I no longer watch many of the crime shows (I miss my Shamar Moore fix), news, docudramas and violent movies. I teach about this all day; I do not want to take it home.

7. **Separate work from personal duties**- my hats off to nurses, special ed teachers and assistants, behavioral specials etc., that work all day with children with behavior health challenges and special needs. I caution, if you spend all day in this capacity,

you may not want to foster children with the same high level of need. You never get to "shut off."

8. **Keeping a balance between work and personal life** – try setting a schedule; make an appointment with yourself; or designate space at home for work that is not in your bedroom.

a. Work

   i. <u>Support</u> – are you being supported through supervision or regular check-ins with your colleagues.

   ii. <u>Hours</u> – even if you are an exempt employee, self-employed, or a stay-at-home parent, your 24/7 should not be filled with taking care of things for others.

iii. <u>Workload</u> – are you the overachiever or the one the boss always asks to do extra? Is your workload distributed evenly among your team? Is your workload realistic? Is it time for you to speak up for a change?

b. Home

i. <u>Sleep</u> – do you really know how many hours of sleep you need for optimum functioning? You should find out. You may be getting too much or not enough. I have learned to appreciate a 30-minute power nap in the afternoon on occasion.

ii. <u>Exercise</u> – try to get moving at least 30 minutes per day and get sunlight, it boosts endorphins.

iii. <u>Hydration</u> – it is recommended that every 20 minutes you take a drink of water.

This is neither an exhaustive nor a magical list. Many of these things you have heard of, may be or have been doing, but sometimes we need reminders or new ideas. These are my suggestions based on research and personal experience. Living balanced is key and do not hesitate to seek counseling. Courtesy of Mental Health First Aid, here is one last suggestion:

✣ Self Care

> **R** - Rest
>
> **E** – Eat Right
>
> **C** - Communicate
>
> **H** – Heal
>
> **A** – Accept help
>
> **R** - Respite
>
> **G** – Get enough sleep
>
> **E** - Exercise

Being Trauma-informed

 Realizing the widespread impact of trauma and understanding potential paths for recovery.

 Recognizing signs and symptoms of trauma in clients, families, staff, and others involved with the system.

 Responding by fully integrating the knowledge about trauma into your policy, procedures, and practices.

 Seeking to actively resist re-traumatization.

These tenets provide a framework for practicing trauma-informed engagement strategies. However, before you can practice, you must have a shift in your mind-set. It is not enough to learn the ways and then continue with business as usual if we are trying to affect a change. Most importantly, you as a champion must be trauma-informed with yourself! This is called self-care. Next, we will talk about what self-care is, why people do not participate in self-care and then some strategies for self-care.

Yes, Self-care Is Selfish

The term self-care refers to activities and practices that we can engage in on a regular basis to reduce stress and maintain and enhance our health and well-being.

What Is Self-care?

- Engaging in activities and practices to reduce stress

- Maintaining health and well-being

- Honoring your professional and personal commitments

- Taking care of yourself better than you take care of others

- Reducing your vulnerability

We know you are capable of caring for others, which is the essence of why you are either in the helping profession or have taken on the role of foster/resource parent. But, in all your caring, you neglect to take care of yourself. You do not always use kind words with yourself. You do not make time to spend with yourself doing the things that bring a smile to your face. Why are we so conscious of spending time on others but not ourselves?

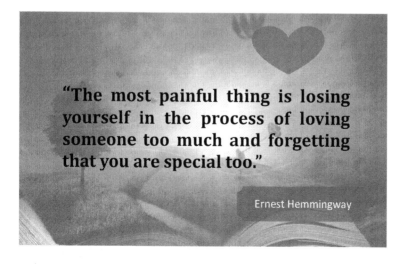

"The most painful thing is losing yourself in the process of loving someone too much and forgetting that you are special too."

Ernest Hemmingway

Why Not Self-care?

We do not engage in self-care as often as we should because we hold some of these beliefs:

- its selfish
- neediness equals real love
- people know how to treat us
- others will take care of us
- we are not worth it

Belief: Self-care Is Selfish

What Does Selfish Mean?

Selfish:

1) of a person, action, or motive lacking consideration for others; concerned chiefly with one's own personal profit or pleasure.

2) arising from concern with one's own welfare or advantage in disregard of others

Self:

1) a person's essential being that distinguishes them from others.

2) sense of who you are, deep down — your identity

ish:

1) a suffix used to form adjectives from nouns, with the sense of belonging to.

2) after the manner of," "having the characteristics of," "like" (babyish; girlish; mulish).

The perception of self-care has a negative connation, however, when combining the prefix and suffix, we translate selfish as "after the manner of or belonging to a sense of who you are." Collectively with the definition of "concerned chiefly with one's own personal profit or pleasure," then we should be selfish.

Belief: Neediness Is Real Love

Our definitions and examples of love come from the dramatization from movies and television. It fosters the belief that love is based on dependence. This sensationalism causes us to be totally focused on the object of our love, therefore forgetting ourselves.

Belief: Others Know How To Treat Us The Way We Want To Be Treated

The truth is people learn how to treat us by watching how we treat ourselves. When we show that we are a rescuer and sacrifice ourselves for others, we attract people who want to be rescued and believe it has to be all about them. This perpetuates a cycle of feeling the rewards of being a rescuer then feeling victimized once the other person no longer needs to be rescued.

Belief: Others Will Take Care Of Us

Sometimes we give of ourselves under the guise of just being nice yet secretly expect something in return. Unconsciously, we become resentful when they did not give back in equal measure. In fact, we have chosen to give all of our love to others and not take care of ourselves. Your self-care is your responsibility, not someone else's.

Belief: We Are Not Worth It

Often it is easy to see the value in others and not ourselves. If we place value in our self-worth by spending the same or greater energy on us than we do on others, then we will attract the same energy from others.

Being kind to yourself is not the end all of self-care. I would like to invite you to consider being more mindful in the way you tend to yourself physically, emotionally and mentally. This is essential to recovering from vicarious trauma. Specifically, it is most effective to include strategies which provide balance, healthy habits, limits and connections with others. Nurturing yourself with activities that:

- provide an escape
- promote mindfulness
- focus on pleasure and comfort as well as play

When was the last time you played? I asked this question to a group of adults and someone asked, "What do you mean by play?" I told her, "If you are asking, then you have not played in a long time." Playing is doing something you enjoy that brings a smile to your face while you are doing it. We play with the children but when did you last play as an adult doing what you wanted to do without the children? If you like to hike or walk, do you splash in the water puddle? Do you play board games with your friends? Do you have date nights and go to the arcade? It is okay for adults to play, have fun, and enjoy life without the children.

Benefits of Play

Let's play a game of true or false, is this a benefit of play?

1. Reduces stress?	True ___ or False ___
1. Dulls brain function?	True ___ or False ___
3. Boosts creativity?	True ___ or False ___
4. Reduces interaction in relationships?	True ___ or False ___
5. Keeps you feeling young and energetic?	True ___ or False ___

Answers: 1, 3, and 5 are true; 2 and 4 are false

1. **Reduced stress.** Playing can trigger the release of endorphins, the body's natural feel-good chemicals. Endorphins promote an overall sense of well-being and can even temporarily relieve pain.

2. **Improve brain function.** Playing chess, solving puzzles, or activities that challenge the brain can help prevent memory problems and improve brain function. The social interaction of playing with family and friends can also help ward off stress and depression.

3. **Stimulate the mind and boost creativity.** Adults, much like children often learn best when they are playing. You learn a new task better when it's fun and you're in a relaxed and playful mood. Play can also stimulate your imagination, helping you adapt and solve problems.

4. **Improve relationships and your connection to others.** Sharing laughter and fun can foster empathy, compassion, trust, and intimacy with others. Play doesn't have to include a specific activity; it can also be a state of mind. Developing a playful nature can help you loosen up in stressful situations, break the ice with strangers, and form new relationships.

5. **Keep you feeling young and energetic.** Play can boost your energy and vitality and even improve your resistance to disease, helping you function at your best.

> "We don't stop playing because we grow old; we grow old because we stop playing."
>
> George Bernard Shaw

While we are addressing the exposure to trauma in your professional environment, self-care involves maintaining balance. Strategies for healing should include intervention in your personal, professional, and family spheres.

Activity: Balancing Mindfulness

Use the Mindfulness Wheel to make a list of ways you can be more mindful in your engagement with yourself and others. Please consider these four categories: Self, family, friends, and work. I have provided a sample activity for each category. Please feel free to change it or add to the list. There is also a blank copy of this activity for you to copy in the Handouts section of the book.

Mindfulness Wheel

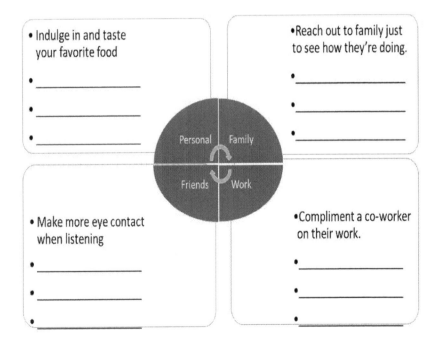

Activity: PERSONAL RESOURCES

Sometimes our biggest stressor is not knowing who or where to go to for help.

Instructions: Make a list of your current resources that are hope-giving, spirit-renewing, creative, playful, loving, affirming. Who or what do you go to that make you feel better?

Resource Needed	Where do I go to meet the need?
Internal (thoughts/beliefs/ affirmations)	
External (practices/sounds	
People	
Places	
My body/My Health	
Laughter	

Healing From Vicarious Trauma

The process of healing cannot be done in isolation. Just as in your role working with trauma survivors, you have seen and believe healing is possible, you believe heroism is just as real as villainy. You have been the hero to others, it's important to find your hero and healer.

1. **Educate** yourself and others on second-hand shock.

2. **Work collaboratively to check-in** with each other as either caregivers, or colleagues. If you are in a supervisory role, create a space for workers to discuss feeling associated with their work. Sample discussion questions may include:

   a. How is staff being affected by their trauma work?

   b. How do they feel about it?

   c. What will we do as a team/organization about it?

3. **Create a realistic** daily, weekly, and monthly schedule that builds in time for breaks (including exercise and rest), and spreads your workload evenly between varied tasks (i.e., meetings, appointments, and education)

4. **Communicate** – do not holding your feelings inside. Practice the techniques you share with your children

or clients. Find a healthy outlet such as a support group or therapist.

5. **Create a transition strategy** for home-to-work and work-to-home. This may include playing music, changing clothes, or sitting still for ten minutes or creating what I call a "to-don't list." I use the to-don't list as an opening activity for many of my classes. We are often distracted by the things we need to do at the time we cannot do anything about them.

Instructions for the "to-don't list

a. **From home-to-work:** Take one minute to write a list of things that may have you distracted or not fully present going into your workday (i.e., groceries, appointments to make). Stash the list somewhere that you will not see until time to go home.

b. **From work-to-home:** Take one minute to write a list of work items that you need to leave at work (ie., incomplete tasks, conflict with colleague, or unsettling interaction with a client). Place that list somewhere in your office to get back to it the next day.

6. **Make a commitment** to addressing second-hand shock. Start with one change at a time.

Lastly, hugs are a no-cost healing strategy. Do you recall the radio commercial by Kaiser Permanente on the health benefits of hugs? You should look it up.

Strategies I will use for my healing:

1. _____

2. _____

3. _____

Who can I include on my collaborative team?

_____

Activity: What Is Your Kryptonite?

Check your undershirt, does it have an "S" on it? If your answer is something other than "no," there is a different book for you to read. While you may desire to, it is not your charge to help everyone. Even Superman has kryptonite aka limitations or something that will impede his mission.

What is your kryptonite or thing(s) you should avoid that may propel you into second-hand shock (e.g., not being able to say "no," or juggling too much, or picking up the slack of coworkers, or diet, or not getting enough sleep?_____

_____

_____

How do you recharge after being disarmed by your kryptonite?

_____

_____

What can you do differently? _____

_____

_____

Who can you go to for help? _____

_____

_____

Activity: Re-engage Your Sense

- When was the last time you took a break?
- Do you know what a rose really smells like?

Vicarious Trauma can cause your senses to become dull. The next time you take your break, think of ways you can be more mindful. Practice being mindful of the way things smell, how they feel, what they sound like, what they taste like, what colors you see. For example, select a route you don't usually travel; notice what foliage is present and its colors and smells. What sounds do you hear along the route? When you go to the snack shop for a drink, notice the temperature of the beverage, is it too cold, too warm, or just right? What fruits do you taste specifically? Take a moment to write down your experience in the card below. I would like to challenge you to complete the whole card and use this as a continual reminder. I have included more of these cards in the *handouts* section for future use.

Which sense(s) did you engage and how? Date: _____	
Sight	
Smell	
Taste	
Touch	
Sound	

Activity: Heart, Mind and Feet

Now that you have some information on being empathetically trauma-informed, let's look at how you will use this knowledge personally and in your program:

1. Some things I will take to heart:

_____

_____

_____

2. Some things I will bear in mind:

_____

_____

_____

3. Some things I will put feet to (take action):

_____

_____

_____

Handouts

Handouts

Which sense(s) did you engage and how? Date: _____	
Sight	
Smell	
Taste	
Touch	
Sound	

Which sense(s) did you engage and how? Date: _____	
Sight	
Smell	
Taste	
Touch	
Sound	

Handouts

Mindfulness Wheel

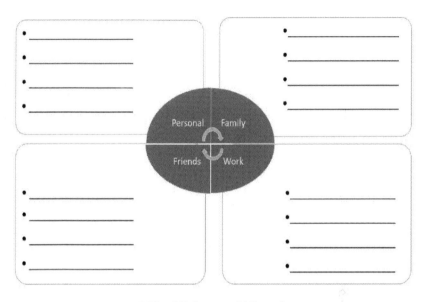

Mindfulness Wheel

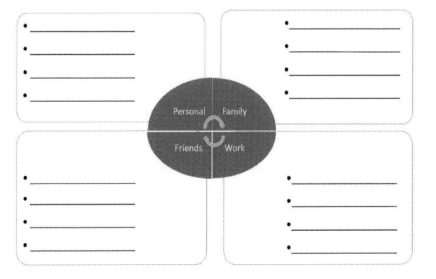

Handouts

Self-care Assessment

Adapted from Saakvitne, Pearlman, & Staff of TSI/CAAP (1996). Transforming the pain: A workbook on vicarious traumatization. Norton

Feel free to rate yourself on how often and how well you are taking care of yourself. When you are finished, look for patterns in your responses. Are you more active in some areas of self-care but ignore others? Are there items on the list that make you think, "I would never do that"? Listen to your inner responses, your internal dialogue about self-care and making yourself a priority. Take note of anything you would like to include more in your life.

Rate the following areas based on how well you think you are doing

3 = I do this well (e.g., frequently)
2 = I do this OK (e.g., occasionally)
1 = I barely or rarely do this
0 = I never do this
? = This never occurred to me

Physical Self-Care

_____ Eat regularly (e.g. breakfast, lunch, and dinner)
_____ Eat healthily
_____ Exercise
_____ Get regular medical care for prevention or when needed
_____ Take time off when sick
_____ Get massages
_____ Dance, swim, walk, run, sing, or do other fun physical activity
_____ Take time to be sexual - with myself, with a partner
_____ Get enough sleep
_____ Wear clothes I like
_____ Take vacations

Psychological Self-Care
____ Take day trips or mini vacations
____ Make time away from telephones, email, and the Internet
____ Make time for self-reflection
____ Notice my inner experience - listen to my thoughts, beliefs, attitudes, feelings
____ Have my own personal psychotherapy
____ Write in a journal
____ Read literature that is unrelated to work
____ Do something at which I am not expert or in charge
____ Attend to minimizing stress in my life
____ Engage my intelligence in a new area, e.g., go to an art show, sports event, theatre
____ Be curious
____ Say no to extra responsibilities sometimes

Emotional Self-Care
____ Spend time with others whose company I enjoy
____ Stay in contact with important people in my life
____ Give myself affirmations, praise myself
____ Love myself
____ Re-read favorite books, re-view favorite movies
____ Identify comforting activities, objects, people, places and seek them out
____ Allow myself to cry
____ Find things that make me laugh
____ Express my outrage in social action, letters, donations, marches, protests

Spiritual Self-Care
____ Make time for reflection
____ Spend time in nature
____ Find a spiritual connection or community
____ Be open to inspiration

____ Cherish my optimism and hope
____ Be aware of non-material aspects of life
____ Try at times not to be in charge or the expert
____ Be open to not knowing
____ Identify what's meaningful to and notice its place in my life
____ Meditate
____ Have experiences of awe
____ Contribute to causes in which I believe
____ Read inspirational literature or listen to inspirational talks/ music

Relationship Self-Care
____ Schedule regular dates with my partner or spouse
____ Schedule regular activities with my children
____ Make time to see friends
____ Call, check on, or see my relatives and friends
____ Spend time with my companion animals
____ Make time to reply to personal emails/letters; send cards
____ Allow others to do things for me
____ Enlarge my social circle
____ Ask for help when I need it
____ Share a fear, hope, or secret with someone I trust

Workplace or Professional Self-Care
____ Take a break during the workday (e.g., lunch)
____ Take time to chat with co-workers
____ Make quiet time to complete tasks
____ Identify projects or tasks that are exciting and rewarding
____ Set limits with clients and colleagues
____ Balance my caseload so that no one day or part of a day is "too much"
____ Arrange workspace so it is comfortable and comforting
____ Get regular supervision or consultation
____ Negotiate for my needs (benefits, pay raise)

Handouts

Self-care practices

1. Identifying negative self-talk and changing it to positive.

2. Pausing before reacting – do I really want to do this?

3. Getting one thing done every day and celebrating this achievement.

4. Being grateful- starting or ending each day with at least three things I am thankful for.

5. Laughing more and starting the day with a smile

6. Singing or dancing whenever possible

7. Having more fun and taking life less seriously.

8. Being my authentic self, not what others want me to be

9. Avoiding over-analyzing a situation

10. Limit my time on social media

11. Not worrying about what other people think about me

12. My self-development, no matter how challenging

Handouts

Foods to promote wellness

Green Tea

- Fights cancer
- Lowers cholesterol
- Prevents cavities
- Protects against heart disease
- Speeds metabolism
- Prevents diabetes
- Antiviral agent
- Maintains a healthy circulatory system
- Strengthens tooth enamel

- Reduces plaque and bacteria in your mouth
- Prevents dementia
- Full of antioxidants
- Prevents food poisoning
- Gives healthy skin
- Prevents bad breath
- Detoxifies

Natural Cure for
MENSTRUAL CRAMPS

Sip chamomile tea to help relax the uterus by elevating the body's levels of glycine, an amino acid that stops muscle spasms.

Try one to three cups a day of the caffeine-free tea during the menstrual cycle.

mavocado.com

Handouts

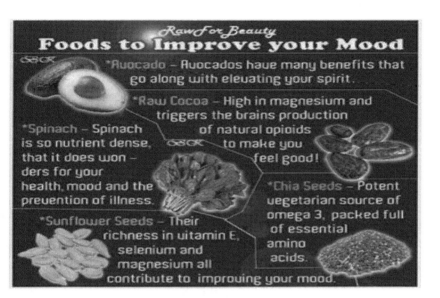

In Closing

Thank you for continuing to support yourself and others during these traumatic times. I hope the words on these pages and the reflective activities are inspirational to you and strengthen you to continue your fight of advocacy and healing for trauma-survivors. You are invaluable in the lives of so many. Remember, it is ok to be selfish in a healthy way.

Thank you for reading my book.

I would like to hear from you. I need your feedback to make the next version of this book and future books better.

Please leave reviews on Amazon, send me an email or visit my website. As a thank you for purchasing the book, please visit my website and sign up to access:
- a free download of the e-book
- exclusive access to on-line workshops
- a free thirty-minute consultation on implementing trauma-informed principles within your agency
- for exclusive discounts

Books are available for purchase on Amazon.com and on my website.

Best wishes,
Theresa Reed
Website: **www.TheresaReed.org**
Email: TheresaReed@outlook.com
Like and follow me on social media:
f Theresareed
f itsnotDrama Itstrauma or   @itsnotDramaitsTrauma
⊙ @itsnotdramaits

Made in the USA
Columbia, SC
21 October 2020

23267648R00048

It's Not Drama, It's Vicarious Trau___ ___ ___he series, *It's Not Drama, It's Tra___* ___ ___on enlightening readers on the effects ___ ___ ___the examination of behaviors that m___ ___ ___as dramatic but are manifestations of ___ ___his edition is a guidebook to recogniz___ ___ ___ing from the effects of second-hand shock syndrome.. Symptoms of vicarious trauma may result in the loss of the passion that propelled us to begin interceding for others. We can become so involved and overwhelmed with helping others that we forget to take care of ourselves.

Based on personal experience in working within child welfare, I am aware of the high occurrence of vicarious and secondary traumatic stress. So, this book is an ode to foster/resource parents and the champions committed to the healing of foster youth and others impacted by trauma.

Theresa Reed is a former foster child who is a passionate facilitator of Learning. With an M.Ed iand Doctoraal candidacy in Adult Education and Learning,, certifications in trauma, Mental Health First Aid and Attachment, Regulation and Competency, plus 15+ years working with Foster/Kinship Care Education and foster youth support programs, she brings a wealth of knowledge.

ISBN 9781734567908

PROGNOSIS

DECOLONIAL POETIC EXHALE //
DESCARGA POÉTICA DECOLONIAL.

BY
BOCAFLOJA

LITERARY TRANSCREATION BY
SIDONY O'NEAL